Sergei Udovik

K Y I V

Photo Album with enclosed Tourist

Vakler
Kyiv
2005

Introduction

Though in 1996 a new spelling for the name of Ukraine's capital Kyiv was introduced, following the Ukrainian pronunciation and spelling, in the album the previous one — Kiev — has been preserved as more familiar to the public.

Kiev occupies a special place among cities of the world. It is not only the largest political, economic and cultural centre of Eastern Europe — not many cities of the world had the honour to become the cradle of one of the world's civilizations, Slavonic-Orthodox — but Kiev has also one more merit: irreplaceable charm, created by a unique combination of picturesque hills, endless Dnieper expanses, and golden domed churches nestled among verdant fields.

Kiev is an astonishing city of light. It is open to sun, sky and water and possesses a strong positive energy.

Kiev is located on the boundary of vast endless forests beginning in France and stretching across the rolling plains, or "steppes" to China. Forest and steppe, high right bank and low left bank, the West and the East meet in Kiev and combine in harmony facilitated by the great Dnieper. The river divides and unifies the city creating a number of channels within Kiev and shapes landscapes of staggering beauty, which can be observed enchantingly for hours from tie high right bank.

There are doors open for you in Kiev in many Orthodox churches that coexist peacefully with churches of other Christian denominations "Catholic, Greek-Catholic, Protestant, as well as synagogues, mosques and other houses of worship. In Kiev you can also see the most ancient Orthodox monasteries. The most famous is the Kiev-Pechersk Lavra — one of the greatest monasteries in the world. Kiev is called the mother of Russian cities, and Kiev-Pechersk Lavra is called the mother of Russian monasteries.

Kiev is also considered to be a spiritual-mystical city. Apparently this environment promoted the shaping of a philosophical world view among Kievites. The famous religious philosophers Nikolai Byerdyayev and Lev Shestov were born in Kiev.

The location of Kiev between East and West created a multicultural atmosphere of tolerance, benevolence

◄ View of the Vydubetskiy Monastery (XIth-XIXth cc.)
from the Botanical garden

The Parkovy Pedestrian Bridge across the Dnieper River

and hospitality. At the same time Kiev is a very modern city, which closely grasps the trends of world development. It is here that a strong scientific potential is concentrated. Modern communications connect Kiev with all corners of the world.

One of the unique features of Kiev is that in a city of three million people you can easily seclude yourself within nature — either in one of the numerous parks or gardens which are spread throughout the city, or near lakes or forest parks surrounding Kiev. Thus Kiev is called a garden city, a city where it is possible to easily combine business life with relaxation. The city spreads its embrace to tourists and businessmen in all seasons — in winter, when there are sparkling golden cupolas against the background of glaringly white snow; or in autumn, when numerous parks are covered in gold and crimson, and yellow and red leaves rustle delightfully underfoot.

But it is especially magnificent in spring, in May, when lilacs bloom, when magnolias exude their fragrance under the open sky, and the chestnut-beauties spread open their flower-candle blossoms. Those who visit Kiev in May retain an indelible sensation of contact with the divine for the rest of their lives, because only God could create such miraculous beauty.

The History of Kiev

The history of Kiev is lost in the depth of centuries. The first settlements of people appeared at the end of the Stone Age about 20 thousand years ago in the region of present-day Kiev. One of these sites, **Kirillovskaya**, named after one of Kiev's streets, contained the bones of 67 specimens of mammoths. Models of dwellings of ancient settlers are exhibited in the **National Scientific Museum of Natural History**.

There are excavated settlements of the highly developed Tripol'skaya culture dating back three thousand years B.C. in the region of Kiev. Contemporary to the Shumyerskaya civilization, it still keeps many mysteries, especially concerning its origins and its disappearance.

According to legend Kiev was founded by three brothers: *Kiy, Shchyek* and *Khoriv* and their sister *Lybyed'*. The city was named after the eldest brother, Kiy. A Shchekavitsa hill in Kiev was named after the second brother, Shchyek, and another hill, *Khoryevitsa*, was named after the third brother, Khoriv. The **river Lybyed'** in Kiev was named in honour of their sister. There is a monument dedicated to the founders of Kiev by the sculptor V. Boroday and the architect N. Fyeshchyenko.

View of the left bank of the Dnieper River from Pechersk

Kiev-Pechersk Lavra Church of the Nativity of the Most-Holy Mother of God and the Bell Tower at the Far Caves →

Historians ascribe the founding of the city to the time around V-VI centuries. An uninterrupted history of the city can be traced from that period on. By the end of X century the city became the capital of a powerful state, Kiev Rus', and an influential political centre of Europe. The wealth and influence of Kiev was connected to trade. It was located on the crossroads of international trading routes, the legendary one "from the Varangians to the Greeks", i.e. from the Baltic Sea to Constantinople, and the second major route, from Regensburg through Prague, Kiev, and further on to Asia Minor and Persia. Kiev was also actively engaged in commerce with England.

The numerous family relations of Kiev princes with the reigning houses of Europe are evidence of the influence and importance of Kiev. Princess Anna, sister of Byzantine emperors, refused Emperor Otto II in favour of *Prince Vladimir* (980-1015), the Baptiser of Rus'. Kiev *Prince Yaroslav the Wise* (1019-1054) was married to the daughter of the Swedish king, and his son Vsyevolod I to the daughter of the Byzantine Emperor Constantin Monomakh. The daughter of Yaroslav the Wise, Yelizavyeta, married Norwegian Prince Harald, who composed songs in her honour. Scandinavian sagas poetically extol how the young man in love flew in his thoughts to the "Russian beauty" and won her hand. Anastasiya married Andrei of Hungary, and Anna, the French King Henri I. After his death Anna governed France as regent and came to be known in French history as Anna of Russia, the Queen of France Anne de Russie Reine de France). *Prince Vladimir Monomakh* (1113-1125) was married to the daughter of the English king.

In XI century in Kiev there were 400 churches, 8 markets and 50, 000 inhabitants, that is, more than in London or Hamburg, where only 20, 000 people lived. Of the West European cities, Kiev was only smaller than Paris which had 100, 000 inhabitants.

Khan Baty, having seen Kiev from a mountain now called **Baty Mountain**, was struck with the greatness and beauty of the city. For 10 weeks Kievites heroically battled the countless troops of Baty, however they could, "not chew" through the **Golden Gates**. The Mongol-Tatars managed to break through the most powerful fortifications of Kiev only at a side of the gates located in the northern part of the present-day area of **Independence Square**, which at that time was covered

St. Nicholas Church at Askold's Grave (1810).
In 882 Varangian prince Oleg killed Kievan
Princes Askold and Dir at this place

Entrance door to St. Vladimir Cathedral.
St. Prince Vladimir Equal to the Apostles and Princess Olha

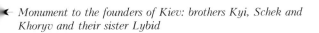

Monument to the founders of Kiev: brothers Kyi, Schek and Khoryv and their sister Lybid

National Museum of History of Ukraine with the remains of the foundation of the Desiatinnaya Church (X thc).

Fortification wall around the Near Caves of Kiev Pechersk Lavra

The Church of the Dormition of the Mother of God (Pyrogoscha), at the background is the Bell Tower of Florovskiy Convent (1740-1821)

with forests and marshes. But even then Kievites did not surrender, but continued to protect their beloved city up to the last citadel, the strong stone Desiatinnaya Cathedral of the Mother of God which had been constructed in the year 980. However the Mongol-Tatars succeeded in destroying its walls with catapults. The cathedral collapsed, and under its ruins a multitude of people was buried. To this day the foundation of the Desiatinnaya Church reminds us of these events. And by the **ruins of the cathedral** the yearly blossoming of the majestic **linden tree** for more than 400 years reminds us of the heroism of the people of Kiev. The invasion of the Mongol-Tatars in the year 1240 brought about an irreparable loss of power to Kiev. Enraged at the up to then unprecedented resistance by the defenders of Kiev, the Mongol-Tatars ruthlessly plundered and destroyed the city. Thereafter life in Kiev slowed down for a long time, and the upper city was left to lie in ruins. Having protected Europe from Mongol-Tatars, Kiev Rus' became dependent on the Horde for many years.

Life in Kiev began to recover only in the second half of XIV century after entering into the structure of the Great Lithuanian Principality. For three centuries, Kiev carried out the important strategic role of protecting the territories of the Great Lithuanian Principality, and after 1569 also the Polish Lithuanian Commonwealth, from the cruel and ruthless attacks of the Golden Horde and the Crimean Khanate armies. Kiev was called the "gate to the entire Lithuanian state". In XVII century, protected by Cossacks, Kiev begins to actively rebuild and restore its numerous churches and monasteries. *Hetman Mazepa* was especially prominent in the field of church building. With his own funds he restored the **Kiev-Pechersk Lavra** and surrounded it with a six meter high strong stone wall. It also served as a fortress wall, thus transforming the Lavra into a citadel. With the assistance of Hetman Mazepa the **Holy Gates** and the **Farming Gates** were built with the **All Saints Church** (1696-1698) above them; you can see the Hetman's family **coat-of-arms** on its facade. With the Hetman's efforts the uniquely beautiful and grand Church of St. Nicholas was built in the Pustynno-Nikolayevskiy Monastery. Unfortunately, it was completely destroyed during the time of Stalin. **Mazepa's house** still stands in Kiev, and the **Hetman Museum** is now located there.

The construction of the mighty **Pechersk fortress** started at the beginning of XVIII century. Most buildings of this complex still stand to this day. Among them one needs to point out the **Moscow Gates**, which led to the fortress from the south, and the **Nikol'skiy Gates**, the **Arsenal**, the **Gunpowder Magazine cellars**,

Upper Moscow Gates (1765)

Nikolskyie Gates (1846-1850)

Fortification wall around the Far Caves (1844-1848)

and the **Vasil'kovskiy** and **Hospital fortifications**. At the present time on the grounds of the latter are a military hospital and a defence installation, **Kosoy Kaponir**, which now houses a great museum dedicated to the Kiev-Pechersk fortress.

In the middle of XVIII century the majestic buildings of the **Sophia** (1740's) and **Lavra** (1731-45) **bell towers**, the complex of buildings at the **Florovskiy Monastery**, the **Pokrovskaya Church** (1766), the **Gostinny Dvor** in Podol and many others were built.

In the second half of XVIII century, after victories in several Russian-Turkish wars against the Ottoman Empire, the Southern Ukrainian territories were added to Ukraine. Kiev became the centre of the south-western frontier of the Russian Empire and entered a new period of development. In 1797 the "Magdeburg Law" was re-established in Kiev. It is the right of self-rule, which the city possessed since the end of XV century. In honour of this event, the **monument of the Magdeburg Law** was built in 1808 in Kiev near the Dnieper River at the place where Prince Vladimir

baptised his sons. International trade was booming, and in 1815-1817 the Trade House was built as the centre of Kiev's trade fairs. It still graces **Podol**. Brokers and Notaries would gather here. On the second floor was a concert hall, where *Angelica Catalini* sang and *Franz Liszt* performed. *Taras Shevchenko, A. Pushkin, N. Gogol', A. Mitskyevich,* and *Honore de Balzac* had visited this concert hall. The latter called Kiev the eternal city of the North, Northern Rome. He said: "Even if I had no friends living near Kiev, I would still travel to Kiev because of my interest in literature and ethnography".

Kontractova Square would fill up with small shops on fair days. Many people would crowd into Kiev to visit these fairs. Prices for hotel rooms would increase dramatically, while those who were poorer would sleep in the open air around the **fountain called "Samson"** (1749), which was part of the first water supply to Kiev.

The water would flow here from the springs of the Starokievskiy Hill. There was a legend connected with this fountain which said that a person who drank water

from "Samson" would stay and live in Kiev forever. In the 1930's the fountain was demolished because, it was justified, that it was a source for spreading infections, and since it was impossible to fight off the number of people who wanted to drink from it. Fortunately, it was rebuilt in 1982 in its original form, but the original wood carved statue of Samson is now kept in the **National Art Museum of Ukraine**.

In 1834 the **University** was opened in Kiev. In 1838-1842 the stately building of the **Institute for Girls of Nobility** was built in the late classical style (architect V.I. Beretti). As it was located on a hill next to an adjacent park, the building looks magnificent from the vantage view of Khreshchatyk. Young ladies from noble and merchant families were given an excellent education here. In the 1950's the building was reconstructed into the Cultural Palace with a concert hall for 2000 seats. It was visited by the first cosmonaut *Y. Gagarin*, academician Andrey Sakharov, as well as British *Princess Anne*. A well-designed concert hall, a modern cinema and other places of entertainment are now in this entertainment centre. At the beginning of XIX century Kiev essentially consisted of three independent sectors **Podol**, **Pechersk** and the **Upper City** — each having its own administration. The **Upper City** was administered by the **Sophia** and **Mikhailovskiy monasteries**.

Pechersk was ruled by the general-governor and partly by Kiev-**Pechersk Lavra**.

The Samson Fountain (1748-1749), restored in 1982. There is a sun-dial above the columns oriented to four corners of the earth

The Column of Magdeburg right (the monument commemorating of the baptising of Kiev Rus (1802-1808)

11

Reconstructed St. Michael's Zlatoverkhy Cathedral
(XII-XX centuries)

The Monument to M. Hrushevsky.
At the background Teacher's House,
where in 1917-1918 Ukrainian Central Council sat

Podol was ruled by the magistrate using the right of self-rule. In the 1830's Aleksandrovskaya Street (now **Grushyevskogo Street**, **Vladimirskiy Spusk** and **Sagaydachnogo Street**) and Bibikovskiy Boulevard (now **Shevchenko Boulevard**) were built, uniting these three sectors of the city into one.

As a result of this, a lot of new buildings were constructed on Khreshchatyk, and in the 1870's the administrative centre of Kiev was moved there. Kiev has transformed into the biggest transport junction in Eastern Europe and becomes the Sugar Capital of Europe. In 1905 the **Gosbank (State Bank) office** building was opened. It is now the **National Bank of Ukraine**. The building that was added in 1934 stands out for its exquisite elements of early renaissance architecture. The coat-of-arms of the Kiev, Podol, and Volynsk provinces are displayed on both sides of the portal entrance. Inside the bank is the **Vyedomstvyenny Museum** (treasury), which houses a rich collection of precious gems and valuables as well as different kinds of money that were in circulation in Ukraine. At the end of XIX century and the beginning of XX century the city was developing very rapidly. The population level increased dramatically as well. In 1865 there were only 71, 000 people, whereas in 1913 the number had increased to 600, 000.

In 1898 the **Kiev Polytechnical Institute** (KPI) was established. It is the biggest and the most famous technical institute not only in Ukraine, but also in the world. Nowadays more than 30, 000 students study here. *Sergei Korolyev*, the future famous designer of space ships, studied at the KPI. A very favourable atmosphere was created in Kiev for those who dreamed about the sky and space. Kievites adored aviation. In 1912 *Pyotr Nyestyerov* completed the first "dead loop" in the world under Kiev skies. Today this complex figure of piloting skill is called "Nyestyerov's loop". Pyotr Nyestyerov is buried in Syryetsk Cemetery in Kiev. The creator of the helicopter, *Igor Sikorsky*, built his first flying machines in the workshops of KPI. The "Aviant" corporation located in Kiev manufactures the famous "AN" airplanes, which include the biggest airplanes in the world the "Antey", the "Ruslan" and the "Mriya".

The first electric tram in the Russian Empire begins to run in 1892 in Kiev, and in 1905 the first funicular (cable car) is built. In 1892 the City Merchant's Assembly building is opened. Nowadays, it is used by the Philharmonic Orchestra. Its concert hall has excellent acoustics. Many famous musicians, composers and singers such as *Tchaikovsky*, *Rachmaninov*, *Chaliapin*, *Scriabin*, *Sobinov*, *Gliere*, *Horowitz* and many others performed on its stage. Pope John Paul II met with Kievites here in 2001.

In the yard of KPI
Main Building (1898)

National Bank of Ukraine
(1902-1934)

The funicular (1905)

The Resurrection Church (1824)
at Florovskiy Convent built in the rotunda style

The Intercession of the Virgin Mary Church of the Veil of the Mother of God of at Pokrovskiy Convent (1889)

House of Peter I (late 17th — early 18th cc.)

In 1898 the Solovtsov Theatre opened its door. Now it is known as the *Ukrainian National Drama Theatre* in honor of Ivan Franco. In front of the theatre, at No.5 Franko Square, is the building of the former Kiev Gymnasium No.8, which was built in 1897. The future soloist and choreographer of the French Ballet, the Kievan Sergei (Serge) Lifar' studied there. He created an entire period of French ballet. Love of Kiev is preserved by all Kievites for the rest of their lives wherever destiny leads them. Thus in Sainte Genevieve du Bois near Paris the laconic epitaph "Serge Lifar de Kiev" is chiselled on his tombstone. Nowadays, there is a yearly international ballet artists' competition in Kiev honouring Serge Lifar.

In 1901 the Opera Theatre opened its doors to spectators. It was built in the French Renaissance style with a capacity of 1628 seats. Many famous touring and Kiev artists performed on its stage, such as *Leonid Sobinov, Fyodor Shaliapin, Mattia Battistini*, and *Anatoly Solov'yanyenko*.

The rapid development of Kiev was interrupted by the Civil War. In the course of three years (1918-1920), power in Kiev changed eighteen times. The city became an arena of the bloody war. So many forces tried to conquer the city: whites, Reds, Greens, Germans, Poles, Ukrainian National forces with differing views. It is impossible to mention them all.

For a short time Kiev became the capital of the independent Ukrainian National Republic (UNR), which was governed by the first Ukrainian president *Mikhail Grushyevskiy*. During the Hetmanat time,

The Parkovy Bridge (1904) known as "Devil Bridge" or "The Bridge of loving couples"

which was headed by the Hetman *Pavlo Skoropadskiy* (1918-beginning of 1919), Ukraine was recognised as a nation by thirteen countries. Hetman Pavlo Skoropadskiy had established the Science Academy of Ukraine. *V. Vernadsky* became its president; *A. Krymsky* became its science secretary.

Skoropadskiy had also established the library of the Science Academy, which had 1 million books. There are 15 million units now. In the 1930's the war against religion resulted in the barbarous destruction of many churches and architectural and artistic monuments. The most valuable among these are the destroyed golden-Domed Mikhaylovskiy Cathedral with its unique XI century mosaics and frescoes as well as the Bogoyavlyenskiy Cathedral of the Bratskiy Monastery.

The buildings of **the Golden-Domed Mikhailovskiy Cathedral** were rebuilt and redecorated with new murals at the end of XX century. Only a small number of buildings is left of the **Bratskiy Monastery**, and a revived Kiev-Mohila Academy is now located there.

In the late 1930's there were also plans to blow up **St. Sophia** of Kiev. It was saved only by the intercession of the President of France who reminded Stalin that this was a French shrine as well, since the daughter of Yaroslav Mudry (Yaroslav the Wise) had built this cathedral and became Queen of France. Stalin, who at that time was negotiating the creation of a union with France and Great Britain against fascist Germany, listened to the words of the President. It was in this way that St. Sophia was saved.

Numerous monuments of historical figures were also destroyed, such as the **monument of Princess Olga**. It was recreated in marble only in 1996 in accordance with the original conception of sculptor Ivan Kavalyeridzye. It was not just the monuments and churches that suffered in the 1930's. With clear evidence these years are called the years of the executed-generation and death by starvation in Ukraine. The best representatives of the Ukrainian technical, creative and military intelligentsia as well as many officials of the Church were executed or exiled to hard labour camps.

These dark times in Kiev's history were replaced by even more terrible times — the fascist invasion. The heroic defence of the city lasted for 72 days. But the city could not hold out forever, and the two year long occupation began.

In the summer of 1942 players from the "Dynamo Kiev" football club won a match against a combined team of "Luftwaffe" German fascist soldiers by a score of 5:3. After the game, which became known in history as the "match of death", four football players were executed. In memory of this event a **memorial plaque to the football players of "Dynamo" Kiev** was erected in the stadium "Start".

The whole world knows about the tragedy at **Babiy Yar**. On September 29,1941 during the fascist occupation of Kiev, all Jews of the city were ordered under threat of execution to gather at the corner of **Myel'ni-**

*◄ The Main "Red" building of The National University
named after T.G. Shevchenko (1837-1842)*

*◄ The library of the National Academy of Science of Ukraine.
It contains nearly 15 mln. books and houses
the depositary of the UN*

View of Kiev-Pechersk Lavra from Pechersk landscape park

*Monument to the Princess Olha, Sts. Cyril and Methodius
Equal to the Apostles, and the Holy Apostle Andrew
the First-Called (1911-1996)*

Babiy Yar. The "Menora" monument

Monument to the children that were killed in Babiy Yar in 1941

kova Street (next to the Jewish cemetery). Afterwards they started hounding them with dogs and ordered them to take off all their clothes. After this they chased them with truncheons far into Babiy Yar, and at the edge of the cliff began shooting them with machine guns. Wounded and alive people fell down into the Yar (ravine) while the dead fell on top of them. In just two days, the 29th and 30th of September, 33, 771 people were killed and buried alive. This tragedy of Jewish and Ukrainian people is described in the novel "Babiy Yar" by the Kiev writer *Anatoli Kuznetsov*. Overall more than a hundred thousand Jews were killed as well as tens of thousands of Ukrainians, Russians and representatives of other nationalities. A seven candle "Menorah" memorial was erected near the site of the executions on the 50th year anniversary of the tragedy. A path of sorrow leads to it from the former Jewish cemetery, and every year on the 29th of September it is used for a mourning procession to Babiy Yar.

There were two more concentration camps in Kiev besides Babiy Yar. In one of them alone, Darnitskiy, around 50, 000 prisoners of war were executed. More than 100, 000 people were taken from Kiev for forced labour in Germany. On the 6th of November 1943 Kiev was liberated as a result of a heroic assault across the Dnieper River and fierce battles. These events are described in detail in **the National Museum of the History of the Great Patriotic War**. The numbers show the scale of losses in Kiev. In 1940 before the war the population in Kiev was 930, 000 people, while after the liberation in 1943 only 180, 000 people remained.

Only in the mid 1950's Kiev started to recover from the wounds inflicted by the war.

During the 1960's and 1970's Kiev becomes a powerful scientific centre of the USSR with distinguished scientists such as *V.M. Glushkov, B.E. Paton, N.M. Amosov and A.K. Antonov.*

Institutes of cybernetics, electric welding, super--solid materials and others are at the leading edge of their fields in the scientific world. The second Computing machine (ECM) in the world was created in Kiev. However, the period of stagnation had a pernicious effect on life in Kiev, and the national liberation movement "RUKH" began to gain strength. In 1989-1991 hundreds of thousands of Kievites led by "RUKH" took to the streets of Kiev demanding liberation from the authority of the Communist party.

On the 24th of August 1991, the Ukrainian Parliament (Vyerkhovnaya Rada) proclaims the Declaration of Iindependence of Ukraine, which was confirmed by the all-Ukrainian referendum on the 1st of December 1991. Kiev becomes the capital of the independent state.

Monument "The Motherland"

Monument to Valery Lobanovsky (2003)
the main coach of "Dynamo"
Kiev football team and the National
football team of Ukraine

Monument to film director Sergey Paradzhanov

Monument to the victims of starvation in 1932-1933

Hotel and Shopping Centre at Bessarabka

*New Dwelling Structures at Tower No 2
of Kiev Fortress Vasylkovsky Fortification*

*The past and the present intertwine
harmoniously in Kiev*

*Underground trade centre "Metrograd"
at Bessarabskaya square*

Modern Kiev

Modern Kiev is the largest cultural, scientific, industrial and sports centre of Eastern Europe. The population of the city is 2.65 million and the area is 820 sq. kms. It stretches 42 kms from north to south along the picturesque banks of the Dnieper and 35 kms from east to west. Kiev is divided into ten administrative regions.

Kiev receives its visitors at the international **airport "Borispol"** and local **airport "Zhulyany"**. The largest passenger **railway station (Kiev-Passenger)** is equipped according to the most exacting requirements and consists of two buildings: an old building in the style of constructivism (built in 1927-32, restored in 2001) and a new ultra modern building "Southern Station", constructed in 2001.

Travellers can also arrive in Kiev through **the River Station** located in the central part of Kiev at the edge of the historical area of Kiev — **Podol**. From here it is possible to take a fascinating stroll along the Dnieper through Kiev and admire captivating landscapes.

Visitors can also arrive in the city by bus at the **Central Terminal**. Those who prefer to travel by car can stop in numerous motels and at auto camp sites.

Cultural life in Kiev is extremely varied with very deep musical and theatrical traditions. One can see performances of minstrels and musicians depicted on 11th century frescoes in **St. Sophia Church in Kiev**. Music in Kiev was taught even during the Kiev Rus' period. Anna, the granddaughter of Yaroslav the Wise, opened a school in 1086 where singers were trained.

Building of the Pivdenny (South) railway station (2001)

Interior of the Pivdenny (South) railway station

Open air concert

"The Theatre on the left bank"

 *National Opera House of Ukraine
named after T.G. Shevchenko*

At the present time Kiev has deservedly acquired the reputation of a great theatrical and musical centre. The Kiev ballet and the opera company tour worldwide, and such opera singers as *D. Gnatyuk, E. Miroshnichenko, A. Solov'yanyenko*, tenor *TJ. Kiparyenko-Damanskiy,* baritone *M. Grishko* have obtained worldwide recognition. The famous conductor Vladimir Kozhukhar' led the Kiev Opera.

Besides academic theatres there are many small theatres and theatre-studios in Kiev. Nevertheless, many of them are well-known abroad. For example, the Kievan "Theater on Podol", of which *V. Malakhov* is the director, has repeatedly received prizes at the most prestigious theatrical festivals. The Kiev Conservatory (National Music Academy) was founded in 1913, and is located at the corner of Kreshchatyk and Gorodyetskogo streets. At the conservatory is a concert hall, where well-known international competitions take place. Among the graduates of the conservatory are such well-known singers as *D. Gnatyuk, E. Miroshnichyenko, L. Rudyenko, A. Solov'anyenko, N. Kondratyuk, E. Yarotskaya*, composers *L. Ryevutskiy B. Lietoshiynskiy, E. Stankovich* (who is one of the ten best composers of the world), and the conductor *V. Siryenko.* The outstanding conductor *Styefan Turchak* taught in the conservatory.

The famous pianist virtuoso *Vladimir Horowitz* was born in Kiev in 1903 in the house at M. Kotsyubinskiy Street. Kiev holds an annual international competition of young pianists in his memory. The renowned tenor *Ivan Kozlovskiy* also studied in Kiev.

National Film Studio named after Alexander Dovzhenko is situated in Kiev. Following famous film directors Sergey Paradzhanov, Alexander Dovzhenko and Vasily Bykov worked here. Sergey Paradzhanov made his famous film "Shades of Forgotten Ancestors"(1965) at this studio.

The annual international festival of classical music "Musik-Fest" is held as well in Kiev. Kiev is also famous for its sports traditions. The *Al'bina and Irina Dyeryuginy* school of rhythmic artistic gymnastics in Kiev is known all over the world. The international "Dyeryugina Cup" is held annually in Kiev. "Dynamo Kiev" is invariably considered to be among the elite football teams of Europe. Kievites *Oleg Blokhin*, who held the title "best football player of Europe in 1975", and *Andrei Shevchenko* are both well known in the entire football world.

In Kiev, other kinds of sports such as sports gymnastics, swimming, handball, hockey, basketball, and beach volleyball are also popular. In addition, races of yachts, kayaks and canoes are held each year. In all these sports Kievites have repeatedly achieved high world results.

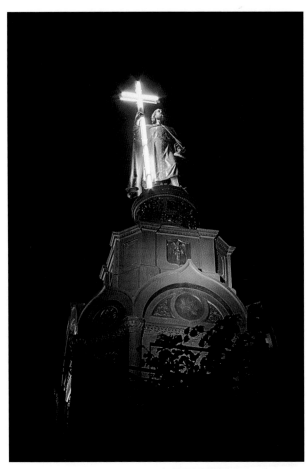

Monument to Prince Vladimir Equal to the Apostles,
the Baptiser of Kiev Rus (at night)

◄— *Monument to Bogdan Khmelnytskiy*
and St. Sophia Cathedral at night

Walks through Kiev

Certainly, the *first walk* should begin on Vladimir-skaya street from the Golden Gates (built 1017-1024), the main entrance to Yaroslav city (1019-1054). In 1983 the **Golden Gate** were restored according to scientific assumptions. Inside are the original ruins of the gates from the time of Yaroslav the Wise. A museum is open here as well as an observation platform from where it is possible to imagine the might of the rampart surrounding ancient Kiev. The length of the rampart extended 3.5 kms with a width at the base of 30 meters and a height of up to 16 meters. The rampart was surrounded by a ditch. The total area of the ancient city was 60 hectares. The **Yaroslav rampart** ran along the same named Yaroslavov Val street up to **Lvov Square**, where the **Lvov Gate** were located. At No. 15 **Yaroslavov Val** street in a courtyard is a conserved building *where Igor Sikorskiy*, the future famous aircraft designer and founder of American helicopter construction, passed his childhood and adolescent years. On the opposite side from the Golden

Zoborovsky Gate (1746). The gates used to be the main entrance to the territory of St. Sophia Monastery

Lime-tree that is more than 400 years old

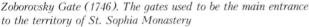

– St. Sophia Cathedral. The main Altar. In the centre — "Unbreakable wall" the mosaics of The Mother of God "Oranta"

Gate the rampart went down to the area of **Independence Square**, where the **Lyadskiye Gates** were located. (At that place there is now an arch decorated in baroque motives). Then the rampart went upwards along **Kostyel'naya** street and in the area of **Mikhailovskaya Square** merged into the rampart of Vladimir city. To the right of the Golden Gate at the corner of No.39 Vladimirskaya street and **Proryeznaya street** stands a magnificent building constructed in 1901. Here there used to be a confectionary store called "Marquisa" mentioned in *Bulgakov's* story "The White Guards".

At No.35 **Vladimirskaya street** the private residence of the architect A. Beretti (1848) was located. And in front of it, in house No. 36 was the Hotel "Prague", where in 1916-18 *Yaroslav Gashyek* lived. It was right here that in the story "The good soldier Svejk in captivity'" came to light, and which then became the beginning of the novel "The good soldier Sveik and his fortunes". At the corner of Vladimirskaya and **Irininskaya streets** you can see a marking outlining the location of the ancient **Irininskaya church** named in honour of the wife of Prince Yaroslav the Wise, Irina (Ingigyerd), daughter of King Olaf. Further along, the street goes into **St. Sophia Square**, where under the bell tower is the main entrance to the St. Sophia courtyard. This area has now been declared a preserve and was included in UNESCO's World Heritage list of monuments in 1990.

The magnificent 76 meter high bell tower together with **St. Sophia of Kiev** creates a baroque ensemble of amazing beauty. A 13 ton bell cast in 1705 still hangs from the second tier of the bell tower. In the preserve area is **a refectory church** named **"Warm Sophia",** a **house for the Metropolitan**, the **St. Sophia Seminary** as well as several museums. The main entrance to the house for the Metropolitan (1722-30) went through the majestic gate called the **Gate of Zaborovskiy**. At the centre of this assemblage is the most unique structure of ancient Rus' architecture, the magnificent 13-domed **St. Sophia Cathedral** (1037). It was named after the Cathedral of St. Sophia in Constantinople (from the Greek word "sophia" which means "wisdom"). It was constructed as the main Metropolitan church of Kiev Rus' in honour of the victory of the ancient Rus' army over pagan nomads and for the glorification of Christianity. A third of all the paintings which adorned the church in ancient Rus' times, that is 260 m^2 of mosaics and about 3, 000 m^2 of frescoes from XI century, is preserved inside the Cathedral. Besides XI century mosaics and frescoes on the cathedral walls one can see works of artists from XVII to XIX centuries. At the zenith of the dome in a medallion design is a mosaic image at Christ the Pantocreator, and around him are four figures of archangels, one of which is a mosaic from the XI century, and the others are painted in oil by M. Vrubyel' in 1884. One hundred and seventy seven shades of mosaics were used for the decoration of the frescoes of the cathedral.

In the vault of the main altar in all its magnificence appears the majestic six meter figure of the **Mother of**

Memorial plaque to the musician and composer F. Liszt

Memorial plaque to the Metropolitan P. Mogyla

Memorial plaque to the designer of helicopter I. Sikorsky

Memorial plaque to the writer Ya. Gashek

Memorial plaque to the Prime Minister of Israel Golda Meir

Golden Gate after the reconstruction

God **"Oranta"** (i.e. praying). This image is called the **"Inviolable Wall"**, as the wall, on which the Mother of God is represented, is indestructible and is preserved in its original condition. It gives the impression that divine force protects it. Kievites believe that this cathedral and the Mother of God "Oranta" in the centre of it are protectors of the city, and as long as the cathedral stands nothing will threaten the city. Standing in the cathedral, you feel an especially calming power. You are overcome with tremors of devotion and a feeling of becoming one with eternity. If St. Sophia makes such an impression on modern man, it is difficult to even imagine the sensations it made on the first visitors to the cathedral.

The burial vault of great princes is found in the cathedral. The **sarcophagus** of **Yaroslav the Wise** and his wife **Irina** is preserved in St. Sophia. The white marble sarcophagus was brought from Byzantium and was probably made as far back as VII to VIII centuries. In the refectory church one can also see X to XI century **sarcophagus of Princess Olga**, which was brought here from the Desyatinnaya Church.

On the second floor of St. Sophia is a unique display of original mosaics and frescoes dating from the beginning of XII century from St. Michael's Golden-Domed Cathedral. A majestic panorama of **St. Michael's Golden-Domed Cathedral** is revealed from the side

View of Podil and panorama across the Dnieper River from the Castle Hill

of St. Sophia Square, and in the foreground stands a **monument to B. Khmelnytskiy** (1881-1888). Continuing the walk on Vladimirskaya, on the right we pass the buildings of former provincial establishments known as "**Prisutstvennye Places**", i.e. offices (1854-1857). Adjacent to this building is a **fire tower** which served as a lookout for suspicious smoke.

On the opposite side of Vladimirskaya street in house No.16 (1879) was a **private hotel**, where the artists *M. Vrubyel'* and *M. Nyestyerov* lived. The outstanding Ukrainian poet and lawyer *Vasyl' Stus* also worked here.

At the intersection of Vladimirskaya and **Bolshaya Zhitomirskaya streets** it is possible to see the red quartz outline of the **foundation of St. Sophia's Gates**, which in turn led into the **city of Vladimir**, the most ancient part of Kiev. At the beginning of Vladimirskaya street it is possible to find a memorial plaque at the site of the **Grand Prince's Palace** (X century), as well as remains of **pagan temples** (X century). While going up to the **National Museum of the History of Ukraine**, we shall see the remains of the foundation of the most ancient stone cathedral of Kiev, Desyatinnaya Church (989-996). Here *Prince Vladimir*, the Baptiser of Rus',

was buried. If you approach the edge of Old Kiev Hill, then the incomparable view of the ancient natural boundaries of **Gonchary** and **Kozhyemyaki** as well as **Zamkovaya hill** will be revealed before you.

On the left rises **Dyetinka hill**. It is here where lovers of meditation and members of spiritual societies come to carry out their activities. The mountain is also revered by Kiev artists, who every May arrange a performance of "Wind Holiday" there. On the right in the distance, vistas of the Dnieper.

Going back to the beginning of Vladimirskaya street, we appear before the outstanding creation by Rastrelli **St. Andrew's Church**. It stands at the top of Andrew Hill. In the most ancient Russian chronicle, "The Story of Bygone Days", the legend was written down that Saint Apostle Andrew The First-Called, preaching Christianity, had spent the night on a slope by the Dnieper, and early in the morning climbed a mountain (subsequently named Andrew mountain), erected a cross and uttered to the people: "On these mountains will shine divine grace. There will be a great city, and God will erect many churches here".

The annals inform that St. Andrew's monastery already stood on this place in XI century. While staying

The iconostasis at St. Andrew's Church

St. Andrew's Church (1747-1753)

in Kiev in 1744, *Empress Yelizavyeta Petrovna* placed the first stone in the foundation of the future St. Andrew's Church. The consecration of the church was held in 1767.

The church is executed in the baroque style and is surprisingly in harmony with the surrounding hilly area. During its construction it was necessary to resolve difficult problems in the development and strengthening of the foundation. A complex drainage system was created around the foundation. The height of the five cupola St. Andrew's Church together with the stylobate is 62 meters. The interior decoration, of the church amazes one with its richness. It was carried out with taste and love based upon the design and drawings of the iconostasis by **Rastrelli**. The best St. Petersburg carvers created the iconostasis. Especially impressive are the works of the well-known Russian artist *A. Antropov*: "The Last Supper", "The Assumption of The Mother of God", and altar paintings. The paintings in the church interact harmoniously with the wood carvings, and the gilding creates a unique game of light with a background of turquoise and purple colours. As a whole the refined appearance of the exterior together with the decoration of the interior of the church creates a celebratory, exuberant mood.

From St. Andrew's Church begins Andreevsky Spusk (St. Andrew's Descent), which twists in serpentine fashion between the Kiev hills and ends in Podol.

It is difficult to find any other street in the world which can be compared with Andreevsky Spusk in its picturesque beauty. It was most probably because of this that it was always so beloved by artists. Many well-known artists, sculptors and writers lived here. The most famous of them was *Mikhail Bulgakov*. The little house at No.13 Andreevsky Spusk is called the **"House of Bulgakov"**. He lived in this house from 1906 to 1916 and from 1918 to 1919. And precisely in this house he set the heroes of his story "The White Guards" and the play "The Days of the Turbiny Family". Now, a museum is located there.

Andreevsky Spusk is called Kiev's Montmartre. It is a favoured place of artists, who gather here each year at the end of May during the opening of **"Kiev Days"**. Then the street becomes a place of pilgrimage for tens of thousands of Kievites and visitors to the capital. Traditionally concerts and art festivals are held here, and many picture galleries, souvenir shops, and antique dealers display their wares.

The sensuality which spills over Kiev, the contrasting play of sunlight, the gold of the cupolas, the light spots on buildings and the relief contrasts of green hills was subsequently embodied in the surprising creativity of the genius painter, Kievite *Kazimir Malyevich*. He studied not far from here, in the Drawing School of N.I. Murashko at No.47 Vladimirskaya street.

To the left of the street you go up to the top of **Zamkovaya hill** by a winding **cast-iron staircase**. From

House of Michael Bulhakov. The author settled the Turbiny family in this house (novels "The Days of Turbiny Family" and "The White Guards")

Heroes of Classical Hit Movies "After Two Hares" — Pronia Prokopivna and Holokhvastov

St. Andrew's Church at night

Stairs near the October Palace at night

here there is a picturesque view of St. Andrew's Church with a sweeping vista of the Dnieper in the distance. From the side of the ditch of Gonchary-Kozhyemyaki you can see **Vozdvizhenskaya street**, where in house No.1O *Mikhail Bulgakov* was born. At the beginning of Vozdvizhenskaya street stands the **Krestovozdvizhyen-skaya Church** (1811-1841). In the middle ages you could find a castle on Zamkovaya hill. One does not need a vivid imagination when one looks at the steep incline of this hill to convince oneself of its impregnability. Archaeologists consider that it was right here that the core of the city of Kiev was created. The cemetery of the **Florovsky Monastery** is found on the northern side of Zamkovaya hill.

View on Podol and Behind Dnieper Land from one of the panoramic points in Kiev

On the right side of Andreevsky Spusk next to Bulgakov's house is the building that Kiev writer *Victor Nekrasov*, romantically called the "**Castle of Richard the Lion Heart**". The building stands out with its modern gothic architectural style and monumental facades which are decorated with elements typical of fortresses and castles. To the left of the building, the steep, twisting cast-iron staircase swoop you up to the top of **Uzdykhal'nitsa hill** to the most cherished lookout observation platform for Kievites. From its height it reveals a captivating view of **Podol and Obolon' districts**, **Moskovskiy Bridge**, **Voskryesyenka** and **Troyeshchina districts**. In good weather you can see the Dyesyenka River which flows into the **Chyertoroy Channel**.

The romantic feeling, created on top of the mountain attracts couples in love, who dying from rapture, direct their gazes into the unembraceable distance.

It is well-known that in every self-respecting historical city a **Lysaya Gora** (Bald Mountain) exists, where on sabbath the evil spirit is cast away. In Kiev there were three such mountains. The most beloved by witches was the mountain on the left bank in the area of **Voskryesyenka**. Not only Kievan witches, but also

those from its surroundings flew here over the Dnieper. But this mountain vanished.

Nowadays another historical Lysaya Gora in the region of **Kitayevo** near Kiev has a gloomier claim to fame. Its strong negative energy is well known not only in Kiev, but in all of Eastern Europe. If you want to feel yourself a hero of phantasmagoria as depicted in Bulgakov's novel "The Master and Margarita", then stay on top of this mountain at night. Here phantasmagoria becomes reality. At the same time it is not the recommended that people with weak nerves visit the Bald mountain.

At night Andreevsky Spusk looks much friendlier, but not less magical. From on top of Uzdychal'nitsa hill, the cupola of **St. Andrew's Church** steams, at the bottom, the evening lights in Podol twinkle, and all around the Kievan hills perish in secret silence. Through the nightly silence the outlines of the trees transform themselves into mythological beings, and it seems as right here a Bulgakov's Margarita will fly over you at any moment. At the bottom of Andreevsky Spusk is a unique **"Museum of One Street"**, which is dedicated to Andreevsky Spusk. Here you can be absorbed into the atmosphere at the end of XIX century beginning of XX century and see the world through the eyes of the Artist.

Podol

It is best to start the stroll through Podol from **Kontraktova Ploshchad'** (Contract Square). This is the most ancient square in Podol, the old merchant town, which in the 19th century became part of Kiev. This square is known since the time of Kiev Rus'. In 1132 — 1136 **the Church of the Mother of God Pirogoshchi** was built here. It is mentioned in the heroic epic "The Lay of Igor's Host". This church was the most revered church in Podol. The magistrate of Podol held ceremonies and kept the city records here. The church was demolished in 1935, and in 1998 a new cathedral in the ancient Rus' style was built in the same place. In its entirety the square recreates the trading atmosphere of Podol at the end of the XVIII — beginning of the XIX century.

The harmony of the square is marred by a four story building in the pseudo-classical style, built at the spot where the bell tower of the **Bratskiy (Brotherhood) Monastery** was demolished in the 1930. The College of the **Kiev-Mohila Academy** was reestablished in 1992 in this building. It was the oldest learning academy in Kiev. In 1632 *Peter Mohila* combined the Lavra and the Bratsk schools into the Kiev-Mohila College. It received the legal rights and title of academy in 1701, and in 1819 it was reorganized into the Dukhovnaya (Theological) Academy.

The Kiev academy was the most famous and prestigious learning centre of Eastern Europe. Students from not only Slavic, but also from Western European countries received their fundamental education here. During the course of several centuries the Kiev academy prepared the secular and theological elite of the entire orthodox world.

The old building (1703-1740) together with the **Congregation Church** (1732-1740) and the assembly hall is still there. Philosophical debates and musical events took place here. Opposite this building stands **the statue of the philosopher Skovoroda** (sculptor I. Kavalyeridzye) who in 1738-1742 and 1744-1750 studied at the academy. *A. Byezborod'ko, A. Vyedyel', I. Grigorovich-Barskiy, A. Miloradovich, I. Samoylovich* studied there as well.

In the academy there are several unique buildings from the XVII to the XIX centuries of the destroyed Bratskiy Monastery and which still stand.

On **Kontraktova Ploshchad'** several buildings in a magnificent modern architectural style stand out, as well as the structures of **the Greek-Sinai St. Catherine's**

The Castle of Richard, the Lion Heart

The celebration of the Day of Kiev at Andreevskiy Spusk (descent)

Celebrations at Andreevskiy Spusk

Monastery, which was founded in 1748 by Greek colonists. Also deserving one's attention around Kontraktova Ploshchad' are women's convent **Florovskiy Monastery** (XVI century), **the Church of Nikola Pritisko** (St. Nicolas Church) and **the little house built** at the end of the XVII century, where according to legend *Peter the Great* would stay.

At No.16A Spasskaya Street near Kontraktova Ploshchad' is **the Hetman's Museum**, which is located in the house in which Hetman *Ivan Mazepa* supposedly lived at the beginning of the 18th century. Not far from the museum is **the Nabyeryezhno-Nikol'skaya Church** (1772-1775) constructed in the Ukrainian baroque style. Next to it stands a granite cross bearing an inscription in Ukrainian: "To those, who sacrificed their lives at the altar of Ukraine.

A block away, the surprisingly cosy **Il'inskaya Church**, named in honour of Elias the Prophet, was built in 1692 on the site where the oldest Christian church in Kiev used to stand. The Il'inskaya Church stands at No.2 Pochayninskaya Street, named in memory of the full river Pochaynaya, which during Kiev Rus' times flowed into the Dnieper at this location. Here in the year 945, the representatives of the Kiev Prince Igor took an oath at the signing of the peace treaty with Byzantium.

Next to the Il'inskaya Church is **the Dnieprovskaya-Nabyeryezhnaya** (the Dnieper quay). Scheduled boats, as well as tourist, hotel, and restaurant boats are moored here. Not far away is the **River Port**. Next to it is the Pochtovaya Ploshchad', which gets its name from **the Pochtovaya Station** (1846), from where postal transportation began, and mail coaches were sent out. **The Rozhdyestvyenskaya (The Nativity of Christ) Church** was located on this square, and on 6-7 May 1861 the body of *Taras Shevchenko* was placed there. At first, T. G. Shevchenko was supposed to have been buried on Shchyekavitsa Hill, but afterwards it was decided to bury the poet genius in Kanyev in accordance with his will. The casket was taken along today's **Nabyeryezhnaya (Quay) highway** to the ship leaving from the station not far from the present-day **Metro Bridge**.

The famous Kievan parks are spread out along the Dnieper to the right and going up from the Nabyeryezhnaya highway.

Monument to Taras Shevchenko →

The Bell Tower of the former Greek St. Catherine's Monastery

Il'inskaya Church of St. Elias the Prophet (1692)

Reconstructed Church of the Nativeity of Jesus Christ. The coffin with Taras Shevchenko was placed in this church when he died. To the right — Post Station (1865)

Parks

When you enter the parks of Kiev, you will realize why Kiev is called the garden city. There are so many parks in Kiev that even without trying you can find a quiet little corner or a solitary bench. **Kievan benches** are a special part of the city's life. They are found everywhere, even in the most secluded places. How many dramatic stories would be revealed to us if they could only talk! How many declarations of love! And how many broken hearts were left shattered at their pedestals. But life in Kiev never stops, not even for a second. Kiev was created for love, and Kievan parks celebrate this.

For each Kievite there are around 1,000 square meters of greenery. The city has about 70 parks, many of which have reservoirs. Kievan parks gracefully blend into forest areas and meadow park zones. As a whole, the green zone occupies 383,000 hectares. Within the city, an area of 40 sq. kms. is covered by water, among which are picturesque verdant islands and parks. This combination of hills, greenery and water give Kiev its unique charm.

The first park in Kiev was laid out by the Metropolitan *P. Mohila* in 1631 in the metropolitan court yard in **Golosyeyev**. Several unique **oak trees** as old as 1,000 years are still standing there. The **National ExpoCenter of Ukraine** is in Golosyeyev. And near it, in Pirogovo, is the open-air **Museum of Folk Architecture and Everyday Life in Ukraine**. Here, covering an area of 150 hectares in the midst of a scenic landscape are more than 300 architectural objects of national folk works as well as a collection of 80,000 items of everyday life. All historic-ethnocultural regions of Ukraine are represented here. Some of the cottages and churches are from the 16th-17th centuries. They were carefully removed from various regions in Ukraine and placed in a natural environment maximizing its approximation to the original setting.

The most beloved and visited parks are the terraces along the banks of the Dnieper. Among them is **Vladimir's Hill** and **the memorial to Prince Vladimir** (1853), the baptiser of Rus'. In the year 988, intent on strengthening his regional power Vladimir introduced Christianity as the official religion of the realm.

In the 1740's, **the Tsar's Garden** (now known as the City Garden), was designed according to Rastrelli's plans. Here is **the Mariinsky Palace** (1750-1755) named in honour of *Mariya*, the wife of Tsar Alexander II. This

The best place for the rest —
benches under the chestnut trees

One of the numerous public gardens

◄— *The lake in Kitaevo district*

The Church in the Museum of Folk Architecture and Life (Pirohovo)

Windmills in Pirohovo

Botanical garden in winter

Pirohovo in winter

beautiful blue-and-cream coloured palace is similar in style to the imperial summer estates in St. Petersburg and was designed by *Bartolomeo Rastrelli*, Empress Elizabeth's favourite architect. It is a lovely mixture of Ukrainian and Russian Baroque. Today the palace is used for official ceremonies and is closed to the public. Next to it is **the Verkhovnaya Rada Ukrainy (Ukrainian Parliament)** building and the viewers lookout, which has a clear view of **the Metro Bridge** and the Left Bank.

Another unique park is **the Central Botanical Garden** located in the historical district of **Zvyerints** and **Vydubichy**. Its huge 130 hectare area is saturated with the richest collection of plants, many of which are rare species. The collection encompasses 13,000 different types and varieties. The botanical geographic landscape is represented here "Crimea", "Caucasus", "Far East", and "The Carpathians". In the park is a singular collection of orchids, and the most outstanding for local collectors is the orchid "Dorotis the Beautiful", which in 1980 grew and flowered in an outer space capsule.

Here you can see an unforgettable spectacle: the blossoming of drooping Magnolias with huge white, pink and red fragrant flowers. The effect is magnified when one hears the pealing of the bells of **the St. Trinity Ioninskiy Monastery (Monastery of St. John of Kiev)**, which is located on slightly higher ground.

The special energy of this place has a beneficial effect on the bountiful lilac garden — the pride of the Kiev Botanical Garden. All the blossoming lilac hues from intense violet to blinding white flow in waves and

View of Mariinsky Palace from the park

◄– *Mariinsky Palace, and Building of Verkhovna Rada (Parliament)*

◄– *Central Botanical Gardens. Trinity Church (1871-72) of Ioninskiy Monastery*

◄– *Flower exhibition-show in Pechersk landscape park*

stream down to the **Vydubetskiy Monastery** (XI-XVIII centuries).

These surprising and inimitable landscapes attracted and inspired painters at all times to create thousands of paintings. Vydubetskiy Monastery is also imprinted in the etching of T.G. Shevchenko. Only a few churches of this monastery have survived over the centuries. Among them are **the Mikhaylovskiy (St. Michael's)** (XI century) and **Gyergiyevskiy (St. George)** (1686-1701) Cathedrals whose glowing, golden and azure cupolas give this place an ethereal feeling against the background of the blossoming lilacs.

In **the Botanical Garden** next to the University of Kiev you also find a special collection of plants. The garden was planted in 1839. The oldest palms in Ukraine aged 200 years grow here in a 30 meter high climate controlled greenhouse together with a rare collection of plants.

In **Pechersk Landscape Park** is **the National Museum of the History of the World War II**. Opened in 1981 this memorial complex occupies an area of 10 hectares and incorporates a museum (18 galleries), an eternal memorial flame, plaques honouring "hero-cities" and a display ground for World War II vintage and more recent military equipment. The seven compositions comprising 100 bronze sculptures lining the road to the complex are good examples of traditional Soviet style sculpture with their powerful portrayal of human strength and symbolize the heroic struggle against the fascists. The centre composition of the complex is a gigantic titanium alloy female figure with a sword and shield in her hands intended to symbolize the Soviet "Motherland" — "the Rodina Mat'". The 62 meter high monument was designed by V.Z. Boroday, V.D, Yelizarov and others. The height of the sculpture together with the pedestal is 102 meters, and the entire monument weighs 530 tons. Not only the size of the monument but also its details are noteworthy. For example, the sword alone is 16 meters in length and weighs 12 tons. The museum's exhibits consist of 8,000 objects reflecting various stages and aspects of World War II.

If you are lucky, you can get a glance of Kiev from a height of 92 meters above ground level or 170 meters above the level of the Dnieper. Every year at the Independence Day there is a magic festival — **Flower Exhibition** in the park at the territory of museum.

A **Zoo** that was founded in 1908 is a worth visiting site of Kiev. On the territory of 40 hectares you can find picturesque ponds and lakes, more than 130 species of trees and bushes. Open-air cages and pavilions for birds and animals naturally blend with this beautiful scenery. Lions, tigers, bears and other animals live in natural environment at "The Island of Animals". Pavilions for exotic birds and reptiles are one of the largest in Europe. More than 3,500 animals and 350 species of birds live in Kiev Zoo.

In the summertime, when the sun warms the city streets with heat rising up to 40 degrees Celsius, hundreds of thousands of Kievites make their way to the beaches on the islands of the Dnieper or hide in the cooling lakes which are so numerous in Kiev.

But even here you have a choice — with difficulty you can find a free patch of sand among the dark bronzed bodies, or search for a solitary little spot on the nudist or secluded beaches and sunbathe in the water in complete isolation, and then remember with astonishment that just now you made your way with great effort through the ant hills of people. The most popular beaches — those with full service, those that are free as well as resting places — are found on the **"Gidropark"** island. The beach volleyball world championships were held here. Summer life is a 24 hour event. Open cafes and cosy summer restaurants stretch one after the other and occupy a huge area. Many of them are open 24 hours a day.

Music for all tastes sounds ceaselessly, fireworks flash fleetingly, and if you tire of the noise of the discotheques, you can take a stroll alongside the channels of the Dnieper. From the little bridge which crosses **the Venetian channel**, you can admire the right bank of the city and the spotlight illuminated bell towers of the Lavra Monastery, or complete your night time stroll with a **boat ride along the Dnieper.**

This unity of a large city with its luxuriant nature is the key to the phenomenoncalled Kiev.

The Zoo. "The Animals' Island"

Pirohovo, the Museum of Folk Architecture and Life. The Church of the Veil of the Mother of God, XVIII century

Pavilion at Vladimirskaya Hill

Magnolia in blossom in the Botanical garden

*View of the right
bank of the Dnieper
River and The Lavra
from the Gidropark
at sunset*

47

Holy Trinity Gateway Church over the Holy Gate (1106-08, 1731)

Kiev-Pechersk Lavra

In 1051 monk Anthony who was Ukrainian by origin came back from the Mount Athos with the blessing of The Holy Mountain. After long wanderings he settled in a small secluded cave dug out by Hilarion who later became Metropolitan of Kiev. Other monks started settling around him, so the monastery and **Far Caves of Lavra** appeared. In 1062 St. Anthony, who liked solitude, left the monastery, dug out a cave at the bottom of the nearby hill and founded **Near Caves**, where he lived and was buried in 1071. Monks elected St. Theodosy to be the Father Superior of the monastery. St. Theodosy adopted a strict monastic rule of Greek Studite Monastery known as "Studite Charter" that he received from the Constantinople Patriarch Alexis. Later on this rule was adopted by all the monasteries of Kiev Rus' and St. Theodosy was called the founder of monasticism in Russia. Since then the Cave Monastery became famous all over Russia and was called "The Mother of Russian Monasteries".

Some of Monastery's ascetics chose the life of hermits. They used to dig out small caves and prayed there for the salvation of the world without leaving them for many years. In these caves their souls were leaving their bodies.

Their Holy Relics stay imperishable to our days. The **Holy Relics of Christian Saints** are healing, and the heads of some of the ascetics exhale the chrism. Modern science is not able to explain this phenomenon.

The relics of *St. Anthony, St. Alipy, St. Agapit, St. Damian, St. Nestor the Chronicler* and epic hero *Elias of Murom* are buried in the Caves of Lavra. Up to now 125 burial places of ascetics remain in the caves. This is the reason why Kiev is also called a Holy City.

The caves of Kiev are special sacral areas. There are more than 45 caves in Kiev, beginning with the famous Lavra Caves, after which the monastery Kiev-Pechersk Lavra was called, and ending with less investigated **Zverinets** caves, **Kirilovski** caves, caves in **Kitaevo** and **Pirohovo**, caves next to the **grave of Askold** and many others.

In 1073 the Father Superior St. Theodosy and the bishop Michael laid a **Cathedral named after the Mother of God**. According to the legend, Byzantium stonemasons saw the cathedral in a cloud and came to Kiev to build it. They were told by the Mother of God to bring an icon of the Dormition that she gave them to Kiev. That is why the Cathedral was named after the **Dormition of the Mother of God**.

View of Lavra and Upper Dnieper from a bird's-eye view

Lavra in winter

Church of All Saints (1696-1698) over the Economic Gate and monastery cells.
Farther — Church of Our Saviour at Berestovo (1113-1125)

His Beatitude Vladimir Metropolitan of Kiev and all Ukraine celebrates the Moleben (Thanksgiving Service) on the feast of The Entry of Our Lord into Jerusalem (Palm Sunday) in the Refectory Church of Kiev-Pechersk Lavra

The Divine Liturgy is celebrated by the walls of the Cathedral of the Dormition at the Kiev-Pechersk Lavra on the feast of the Dormition of The Most-Holy Mother of God

The Divine Liturgy at the Church of the Exaltation of the Cross is celebrated in the Far Caves of Kiev-Pechersk Lavra

His Beatitude Vladimir Metropolitan of Kiev and all Ukraine performs The Great Entrance at the Divine Liturgy at the Cathedral of the Dormition at the Kiev-Pechersk Lavra

The Cathedral of the Dormition and the Great Bell Tower at Kiev-Pechersk Lavra

The Cathedral was built on the sight that was marked by nature — it remained dry at night dew. It became the centre of the "Upper Lavra" — part of the monastery that was built above the ground.

For centuries Kiev and Lithuanian princes and high clergy were buried in the Cathedral. In 1632 a famous Ukrainian scientist and poet *P. Beryndp* was buried there, there were also graves of *P. Mohila* (1646), *I. Gizel* (1683). Luxurious marble gravestone was put on the grave of prince *K. I. Ostrozhsky* in 1574.

The Monastery was becoming more and more famous, and in 1159 *Andrew Bogolubsky*, the son of prince Yuri Dolgorukiy, gave the Monastery the title of "Lavra" and the status of Stavropegal and Patriarchal Monastery that put it in the direct subordination to Patriarch. "Lavra" is a Greek word that means "a street" or "a village". This title was given to the biggest and most respected monasteries. By this time Kiev-Pechersk Lavra became the stronghold of Christianity and the major centre of the enlightenment and cultural life.

The writing of Russian chronicles originates from Lavra. In 1113 the *chronicler St. Nestor* finished his renowned old Slavic Chronicle, "The Story of Bygone Days".

Lavra was also the centre for the development of medicine in Kiev Rus'. *St. Agapit, St. Damian* and *St. Peter of Syria* were the famous monastic healers. Here in the XII century prince *Sviatoslav* (known as *Nikolai Sviatosha*) founded the first hospital in Kiev.

Lavra was well known for its icon-painting school that was headed by *St. Alipy* and *St. Gregory*.

In 1615 a **printing house** was founded in the Monastery. In 1626 the first dictionary and in 1674 the first book on history of Ukraine called "Synopsis" were published here. The books contained marvellous engravings and miniatures. You may familiarise yourself with the production of old monastic printing-house in the Museum of Books and Printing that is situated at the territory of Lavra.

Nowadays Lavra is a unique architectural ensemble that was included in the UNESCO World Heritage list.

Holiness and divine beauty of this place leaves a feeling of unity with God.

This feeling is intensified by the Monastery's position on the picturesque Pechersk Hills. There are many viewers lookout sites here which provide a magnificent view of Lavra buildings and the Left Bank of the Dnieper river.

The cupolas of Lavra are gold plated. According to church symbolism, golden colour symbolises golden sunrays and the Holy Spirit. Cupolas are also often painted green. In this case green colour symbolises life, spring and renovation, it consists of two colours: blue — a symbol of the Holy Spirit, and yellow — a symbol of God Son. The golden cupolas signify "the edge of the sun appearing above the horizon". In the fair weather golden Cupola of **Lavra bell** tower that is 96,5 m high was seen from dozens kilometres away. Its shine was the guiding star for many pilgrims who were coming to Lavra to pray to the Saints and to be cleansed from their sins.

The total area of Lavra ensemble is twenty eight hectares. You can find here 120 architectural monuments of XI — XX centuries and 20 churches (apart from the cave churches).

The total length of the caves is more than 1,000 meters. There are two **ancient wells** there that in accordance with the legend were dug by *St. Anthony* and *St. Theodosy*. A church named after the Icon of The Mother of God "The Life-Bearing Spring" was erected next to the wells.

The Church of the **Saviour on Berestovo** is worth mentioning as well. The founder of Moscow, prince *Yuri Dolgoruky*, is buried in this church. The frescos in the church are dated XI — XII centuries. One can find there a unique fresco called "Miraculous Fishing" pained on one of the walls. The size of this fresco is 100 sq. m.

Nowadays Lavra houses a lot of museums at its territory.

It is worth mentioning that Lavra was repeatedly robbed during its long history. Bolsheviks in 1920s and fascists during the World War Two destroyed a great number of invaluable Orthodox sacred objects. Some of them were sold abroad in 1930s. Thus in Los-Angeles Museum of Arts (USA) you can find gold plated Holy Gates made of silver from the **Church of The Nativity of the Most-Holy Mother of God** (1784) and from the **Church of Exaltation of the Cross** (1767).

An Orthodox monastery, Kiev Theological Seminary and Academy are also situated at the territory of Lavra.

Having had a rest from vanity of the world, you can come back to the twenty-four-hour seething life of Khreshchatyk.

– Monks' cells

– The Entrance to the Church of All Saints (XVIIth. beginning XXcc.)

The Church of Our Saviour at Berestove (1113 — 1125)

Tombstone on the grave of Kiev Prince Yuri Dolgoruky, founder of Moscow, who was buried in the Church of Our Saviour at Berestove in 1158

House with Chimeras. Architect V. Horodetsky (1904)

St. Alexander Roman Catholic Church (1817-1842)

Maidan Nezalezhnosti (Independence Square)

Khreshchatyk

Khreschatyk is a central street of Kiev. The street took its name from a ravine with a small spring called Khreschaty that flew on the place of the street before. From the bird's eye view Khreshchatyk looks like a cross. The length of the street is only 1,300 meters but it is well known far beyond the bounds of Kiev. Khreshchatyk is not only a business and administrative centre of the city — it is also the Kievites' favourite place for entertainment and rest. More than 100,000 people gather here for festivals and celebrations. 400,000 Kievites and tourists gathered at Khreshchatyk for the celebration of Millennium.

At the Southern End of the street there is a **Bessarabsky Market** built in 1912 in "Modern" style. Centuries ago there was an open air market here where Bessarabian farmers used to bring their products. Nowadays it is a central city market that offers very good quality products.

Next to the market you can find an old hotel "Palais Royal" that was built hundred years ago. A new modern business centre with a hotel and shopping malls was recently erected between **Basseinaya** and **Bolshaya Vasilkovskaya** streets.

Across from Bessarabskaya Square a beautiful **boulevard Shevchenko** decorated with two lines of Lombardy poplars goes up the hill. The Boulevard starts with the **monument to Lenin** that was erected 1946.

There is also a picturesque boulevard with famous Kiev chestnuts on the odd side of Khreshchatyk Street. Kievites like to spend their free time here sitting on the benches chatting and drinking beer or lemonade. Khreshchatyk is a street of open-air cafes and bars. You can find a lot of them in a quiet **Passage** that was built in 1913-1915. Khreshchatyk never falls asleep. There are a lot of night clubs, casinos and restaurants here.

Irregular cascade building position on the left side of the street gives a unique impression, especially a tower building that closes the perspective of **Bohdan Khmelnitsky** Street and the building **hotel "Ukraina"** that is situated on the hill against the background of **October Concert Hall**. The cascade of fountains at the bottom of the hotel gives the impression of movement, freshness, and lightness especially in hot summer days.

A history of Khreschatyk is a history of experimental construction site. Every 15-20 years the street was undergoing major reconstructions. That is why from the architectural point of view Khreschatyk is an irregular collection of buildings and sculptures of inconceivable styles. It gives the street a distinctive atmosphere of liveliness.

There is also a multi-storeyed **underground Khreschatic** with shops and bistros.

The House with Chimeras that is situated next to Khreshchatyk and designed by Kiev architect *Horodetsky* is one of the most famous buildings that worth seeing. Sculptural decorations of the building were made by an Italian architect E. Salia. At the bottom of "The House with Chimeras" you can find **Ukrainian Drama Theatre named after Ivan Franko** (1896-98).

A nice unusual monument to Yakovenko, famous Ukrainian artist, is situated next to the Franko Theatre in a small cosy park with a XIX century fountain. It seams that he has just sat down to take a break by the fountain with his funny dog.

St. Alexander Roman Catholic Church that was built in 1817-1842 is situated at **Kostiolnaya** street next to the central square called **Maidan Nezalezhnosti** (Independence Square).

A small alleyway goes up from the Independence Square. One can find here a little neat house, where genius Ukrainian poet and painter *Taras Shevchenko* lived in 1846-1847. Today this is **Literature Memorial House-Museum of Taras Shevchenko** (8ª Shevchenko Lane). His personal belongings and painting materials are kept here. This alleyway is named after Taras Shevchenko. Despite eclectic buildings of Khreschatyk it is possible to say that this street has some special magnetism.

Evropeiska Ploschad' (European Square) is situated at the Eastern End of Khreshchatyk. National Philharmonic Theatre and business and exhibition centre "Ukrainian House" are located here.

Maidan Nezalezhnosti (Independence Square) is the centre of Khreschatic and Kiev's main square. During national holidays and celebrations the square turns into an open-air concert site where dozens of thousands of Kievites and tourists gather together to listen to their favourite singers. Military Parades and demonstrations where the President of Ukraine and the members of the Government are present carried out here twice a year at Victory Day and Independence Day.

From November 22nd till December 8th, 2004 Kreshchatyk and Maidain Nezalezhnosti were the epicenter of peaceful 'orange' revolution indented to defend democracy and freedom of Ukraine's citizens.

10 thousand representatives of all regions of Ukraine set up a tent camp along the whole Khreshchatyk. It transformed into the outpost of Ukrainians fighting for democracy and freedom. Hundred thousands of Kyiviates participated in the fight for their constitution rights day after day, night after night. These events are described on the following album pages.

If you walk several hundred meters from Khreshchatyk up the hill, you will find yourself at a quiet **Lipky** district or at cosy parks of the **Upper Town**.

Nevertheless, despite modernism and rapid tempo of modern living Kiev remains the major religious centre of Eastern Europe.

Fountain at Maidan Nezalezhnosti Square

Underground trade centre "The Globe" under Maidan Nezalezhnosti

← *Parade on Independence Day at Maidan Nezalezhnosti*

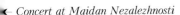

◄ *Concert at Maidan Nezalezhnosti*

Stage at Maidan — Command Post of Orange Revolution. Yulia Timoshenko speaking

Tent Camp in Khreshchatyk

Stage at Maidan at evening. Victor Yushchenko speaking

Tent Camp at Kyiv City Council Hall

Religion

Kiev has always been an Orthodox city. Nevertheless from ancient times it has been tolerant to all world religions. That is why it is sometimes called "Northern Jerusalem". Apart from a great number of Orthodox churches you can find here many other houses of worship, churches and cathedrals where those who practice other religions come to pray.

At **St. Alexander Roman Catholic Church** services are held in Ukrainian, Russian, Polish, French and English. There is also another beautiful **Roman Catholic Church in Kiev named after St. Nicolas** that was built in 1899 — 1909 by architect Horodetsky. The height of the church is 60 meters. Its sculptural decorations were made by an Italian sculptor E. Salia. The church has a wonderful organ; services and concerts are held here. On the Left Bank of the Dnieper River at Voskresenka district a Roman Catholic

The visit of the Pope John Paul II to Kiev

View of St. Nicholas Roman Catholic Church from above

The Interior of St. Nicholas Roman Catholic Church

St. Nicholas Roman Catholic Church (1899 — 1909) →

Chapel of The Holy Apostle Andrew the First-Called (2000)

The oldest synagogue in Kiev (1895)

Lutheran Church

Centre is under the construction. On 27th October 2002 the first stone of the **Ukrainian Greek Catholic Patriarchy Cathedral** named after Resurrection of Jesus Christ was sanctified.

Protestant Church built in 1855 — 1857 can be found at **Luteranskaya Street.** German Evangelist and Lutheran Community of Kiev hold services here. Next to the Church there was a settlement of German Community — descendants of colonists invited to Kiev by Catherine the Great. The Church was named after Saint Catherine who was a Saint Patroness of the Russian Empress. Famous poet and painter *Maksimilian Voloshin* was born in this community of German descendants.

There are also houses of worship of other Protestant Communities in Kiev.

You can also visit the majestic Kiev **synagogues**. Jewish has been living in Kiev since ancient times. The first references to Jewish living in the city are dated X century. Since then synagogues have always existed here.

The oldest remained Jewish synagogue built in Moresque style in 1895 can be found at Podol district. **Kiev chorus synagogue**, which was founded in 1898 and built in the untypical for such type of buildings pseudo-Moresque style, is situated at 13, **Shota Rustaveli** Street. Not far from the synagogue, a building at

5, Basseinaya Street where a girl Golda who later became the prime minister of Israel — *Golda Meir* was born in the family of a carpenter Itsko Mabovitch.

Not far from the synod synagogue (5, Bolshaya Vasilkovskaya Street) in 1887-1990 and 1893-1905 lived a well-known Jewish writer *Sholom-Aleykhem*. While living in Kiev he wrote his genuine novel "Tevje — a milkman". In his novels he described his beloved city of Kiev under the fictitious name "Yegupets" but left originalnames of Kiev streets and cafes.

Muslim Centre and a mosque are under the construction at **Shchekavitsa Hill** at **Lukianovskaya** Street. There is also another mosque at Islamic Cultural Centre at **Dehtiariovskaya** Street.

While being in Kiev Orthodox believers and Roman Catholics have an opportunity to touch the **Holy Relics of Saint Barbara**. Saint Barbara is one of the most revered saints in all the Christian World. She died for faith in 306. The Holy Relics of Saint Barbara were brought to Kiev between 1067-1075 by Byzantine Princess Barbara who married Prince of Kiev Sviatopolk. Previously they were kept in Mykhailivsky Zlatoverkhyi Monastery (Saint Michael's Monastery), and nowadays you can find them at **Saint Vladimir Cathedral**. The Cathedral was built in 1882 in the Byzantine style and consecrated to the 900 Anniversary of Baptising of Russia. The famous architects I. *Shtorm, P. Sparro* and *A. Beretti* were involved in the design works of the Cathedral. Inside the cathedral is grand and spacious, light and richly painted by Russian painters *V. Vasnetsov, M. Nesterov, M. Vrubel,* Ukrainian painters *V. Zamyrailo, S. Kostenko, N. Pymonenko* and Polish painters *P. Svedomsky and V. Kotarbynsky* under the direction of professor *A. Prakhov*. The mosaics of the interior of the Cathedral were made by Venetian masters. The main entrance door was designed by A. Prakhov.

St. Vladimir Cathedral (1862-1882)

The Mosque at Shchekavitsa

— The Interior of St. Vladimir Cathedral
To the right — Relics of St. Barbara

National Art Museum of Ukraine

Museums

Kiev is a city of museums. Some of them have already been mentioned above. It would be impossible to describe all of them and we will tell you about the most notable ones.

The State museum of Taras Shevchenko. The museum is situated at 12, Boulvard Shevchenko. In the XIX century the building belonged to the Mayor of Kiev Demidov, later it became a palace of the outstanding entrepreneur and patron of arts M.A.Tereshchenko. The museum's collection of more than 80 000 exhibits is composed of personal belongings of the poet, his paintings and etchings, copies and original manuscripts of his poems, rare photographs. Beside the above-mentioned House of Shevchenko at the alleyway named after the poet, there is one more building in Kiev at 5, Vishgorodskaya Street, where Shevchenko lived in August 1859. Nowadays this is Memorial House-Museum of Taras Shevchenko. The **National University** is named after the great Ukrainian poet as well and is known as Taras Shevchenko University. On the front wall of the main University building that was built in 1837 — 1842 one can find a memorial plaque to the poet. He wor-ked in this painted dark red building in 1845 — 1847 as a member of the Archaeological Commission.

Opposite the main University building in a picturesque park that was also named after the poet you can find a **monument to Taras Shevchenko** that was erected in 1939.

Museum of Lesya Ukrainka. Lesia Ukrainka (real name Larysa Kosach) is a well-known Ukrainian poetess. The museum is situated at 97, Saksaganskogo Street. Her friend *Olena Pchilka* famous Ukrainian writer lived in this building and Lesia often used to come and stay with her friend between 1899 and 1910. She wrote a lot of her famous poems while being here. The museum collection displays personal belongings of the poetess, manuscripts and first editions of her works. There is a **monument to Lesia Ukrainka** that was erected at the square named after this renowned Ukrainian poetess. Opposite Mariinsky Palace in the park you can find a graceful **sculpture of L. Ukrainka** made by sculptor V. Borodye and architect Ignatenko. Next to it there is also a sculpture of the outstanding Ukrainian actress *Maria Zankovetskaya* made by sculptor G. Kal'chenko. She lived in Kiev at 121, Bolshaya Vasilkovskaya Street, where there is now a **museum**.

Museum of Theatriacal, Musical and Cinema Arts of Ukraine. The museum is situated at the territory of

National Art Museum of Ukraine (namu@i.com.ua). The museum occupies the building, decorated with lions, which was built by architect Horodetsky in 1897-1899 according to the design of P. Boitsov. The sculptural decoration was made by sculptor E. Solia. Different trends in the Ukrainian art are presented in the museum. The museum features a collection of ancient icons, the most valuable of them are "St. George with Life" (XII century) from St. George monastery that is situated not from Sebastopol and the Icon of the Mother of God "The Protecting Veil" (beginning of XIII century). A unique collection of folk paintings of XVIII-XIX centuries can be found in the museum. There is also a collection of portraits of Ukrainian Hetmans and officers of Cossacks Army dated XVIII century. Collection of representatives of Ukrainian avant-garde Ekster, O. Bogomazova, V. Yermilova and others can be seen here as well.

St.George with Scenes from his Life. 11th c. (?). Byzantine state

Crist in Majestry. Latter half of 15th c. Halychyna

Anonymous master. The portrait of Hetman of Ukraine Zinoviy-Bogdan Khmelnytsky. Mid-18th c. B.Khmelnytsky has a mace in his hands. Until 19th c. it had been a symbol of powers of Polish and Ukrainian hetmans. Mace is an ancient weapon used in Western Europe and Russian State since 11th c.

National Museum of Taras Shevchenko in Kiev: T. Shevchenko. Roman-Catholic Cathedral of St.Alexander in Kiev. Watercolour (1846)

T.Shevchenko. Church of All Saints in the Kiev-Pechersk Lavra. Sepia. 1846

M.Vrubel. Girl at Persian Carpet Background

V.Makovsky. Girl in Ukrainian Dress

Kiev Russian Art Museum. White Hall Interiors

Mariinsky Palace. White Hall

B. and V. Khanenko Museum of Arts. Golden Study Room

Quiver Plaque. Scythia. 4th c. BC

Torah-Shield. Ukraine. Odessa. Late 19th c.

Kolts (Hear-Dress Pendants). Ancient Rus. 11th — 13th cc.

Pyx. Kiev. Craftsman — S.Taranovsky (18ᵗʰ c.)

Kiev-Pechersk Lavra. The museum numbers more than 200,000 exhibits of XVIII-XX centuries and owns archives of outstanding representatives of Ukrainian culture — *M. Kropivnytskiy, I. Karpenko-Kariy, P. Saksahanskiy, N. Lysenko* and many others.

Museum of the History of Kiev was opened in 1982 in a famous **Klovskiy Palace** (1753-1755). Its exposition contains nearly 200,000 original exhibits and includes archaeological, culturological, and ethnographic collections. There are collections of icons, artefacts, personal belongings of Kievites of different centuries and good collection of photographs.

Historical Treasures Museum. The museum is situated at the territory of Kiev-Pechersk Lavra at **Kovnirovskiy Building**. The highlight is the display of a golden Scythian pectoral (breast ornament), a silver vase both dated IV century B.C. and other articles of Scythian-Antique Age. There is also an extensive collection of artefacts made of precious stones in VI — XII centuries by Russian masters, collection of jewellery made by Russian goldsmiths in XVI — XIX centuries and a unique collection of Jewish ritual silver (XVIII- beginning of XX centuries).

Museum of Art after Bogdan and Varvara Khanenko. Museum of Art was founded in 1919 on the basis of the private collection of Kiev archeologist Bogdan Khanenko. The Green Cabinet features the collection of Medieval Art, the Golden Cabinet contains objects of Rococo epoch and in the Red Cabinet you can find paintings of Renaissance period. There are 17,000 exhibits in the museum funds. Among the exhibits are the paintings of *J. Bellini, F. Hals, J.-L. David, J. Reynolds, P. P. Rubens, Surbaran,* masterpiece "Infant Margaret" by *D. Velózquez* and unique Byzantine/Sinai icons of VI-VII written by wax paint. Interesting exhibits are presented at the Department of Oriental Art: piece of Coptic fabric with the picture of horseman (V-VI centuries), ritual Chinese bell (I century B.C.), excellent Chinese paintings on the scrolls (XV-XX centuries), Japanese paintings and a rare collection of the details of sword handles (XV-XIX centuries).

Kiev Museum of Russian Art. The museum is situated in the former mansion of *Tereschenko* built in 1882 — 1884. The exposition of the museum has an outstanding collection of Russian icons dated XII — XVIII centuries including a precious icon "Boris and Gleb" and masterpieces by *I. Repin, M. Vrubel, N. Rerikh, I. Aivazovsky, B. Kustodiev, N.Ge, I. Shishkin* and many others.

National Museum of Ukrainian Folk Decorative Art. The museum was opened in the Metropolitan House dated XVIII century and Blahoveshchenskaya (Annunciation) Metropolitan Church dated 1905 at

Museum of T.G. Shevchenko.
Taras Shevchenko lived here in 1846-1847

Museum of Hetmans

Park Sculpture of L. Ukrainka in the city park

Park Sculpture of M. Zankovetska in the city park

the territory of Kiev — Pechersk Lavra. It contains the richest collection of Ukrainian folk art of XV-XX centuries including embroidery, wood carving, ceramics, art glass, china, faience, carpets, pysanky (painted eggs). Special expositions are devoted to painters *Catherina Bilokur* and *Mariya Prymachenko.*

Ukrainian Museum of Book and Book Printing is located in the premises of the former Lavra printing house. The exposition totaling 52 thousand items presents the history of book from Kievan Rus' times till our days. The collection includes unique samples of the 16th-18th cc. Old Printed books from Kiev-Pechersk, Lviv, Ostrih, Univ, Pochaiv, Chernihiv and Moscow printing houses, the first editions of Ukrainian writers and poets.

The Miniatures Museum (at the territory of Kiev-Pechersk Lavra). A unique collection of Ukrainian craftsman *N. Siadrystiy* is presented at the exposition. The works displayed here will hit your imagination. He didn't only managed to shoe a flea, you will also be able to see there a beautiful rose size of which is 0.05 mm that was put inside a well — polished human hair or a model of frigate called "Scarlet Sails" that is 5 mm long. It consists of 337 parts, and rigging is 400 times thinner than a human hair. All these works are hand-made by N. Siadristiy.

Museum of Ukrainian Hetmans. Museum is situated at Spasskaya Street. Separate halls of the museum are dedicated to Hetman *Ivan Mazepa* and Hetman *Pavlo Skoropadskiy.*

Museum "Kirilovskaya Church" (St. Cyril's Church). The church was built in 1146 and was used as a family burial vault of Princes Olgovichi of Chernihov. Prince Sviatoslav Vsevolodovich one of the heroes of chronicle "A Legend on a Regiment of Prince Ihor" was buried in this church in 1194. Here you can see 800m² of frescos of XII century and majestic wall paintings by Vrubel including a famous "The Mother of God with a Baby".

State Aviation Museum. The display includes thirty three exhibits. Among them you can find the following models airplanes — IL, MIG, SU, AN, TU, rare spacimens B-6, B-12, as well as helicopter MI-26. Visitors have an opportunity not only to see and touch the airplanes that reflect the history of Ukrainian aviation but also get into the cockpit.

Chemist's Shop Museum at Podol in the chemist's building dated 1818 — 1820 can be found at Pritysko-Nikolskaya Street. The first chemist's shop in Kiev was opened here in 1728. Laboratory of chemist, cabinet of a healer and a monk's cell were restored and opened for tourists.

On pages 76-77: Touristics Map of City Centre

On the last page: Fireworks over Kiev

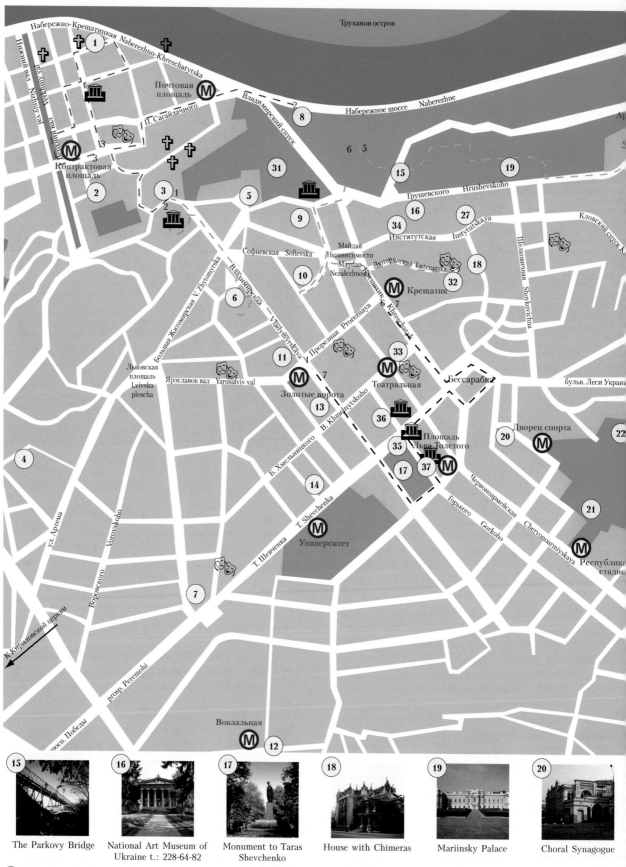

Труханов остров

Набережно-Крещатицкая Naberezhno-Khreschatytska

Нижний вал Nizhniy val

Нижний вал Nizhniy val

Почтовая площадь

П. Сагайдачного

Контрактовая площадь

Владимирский спуск

Набережное шоссе Naberezhne

Грушевского Hrushevskoho

Софиевская Sofievska

Майдан Незалежности Maydan Nezalezhnosti

Институтская

Instytutska

Лютеранская Luteranska

Крещатик Khreschatyk

Крещатик

Большая Житомирская V. Zhytomyrska

Владимирская

Владимирская Vladymyrska

Прорезная Proriznaya

Львовская площадь Lvivska ploscha

Ярославов вал Yaroslaviv val

Золотые ворота

В. Хмельницкого

B. Khmelnytskoho

Театральная

Бессарабка

бульв. Леси Украин

Шелковичная Shovkovichna

Кловский спуск K

Дворец спорта

Площадь Льва Толстого

Б. Хмельницкого

Т. Шевченко T. Shevchenko

Т. Шевченко

Университет

Червоноармейская

Горького Gorkoho

Червоноармейская Chervonoarmiyskaya

Республика стадис

ул. Артема

Воровского Vorovskoho

К Кирилловской церкви

prosp. Peremohi

Воровского

Вокзальная

проеп. Победы

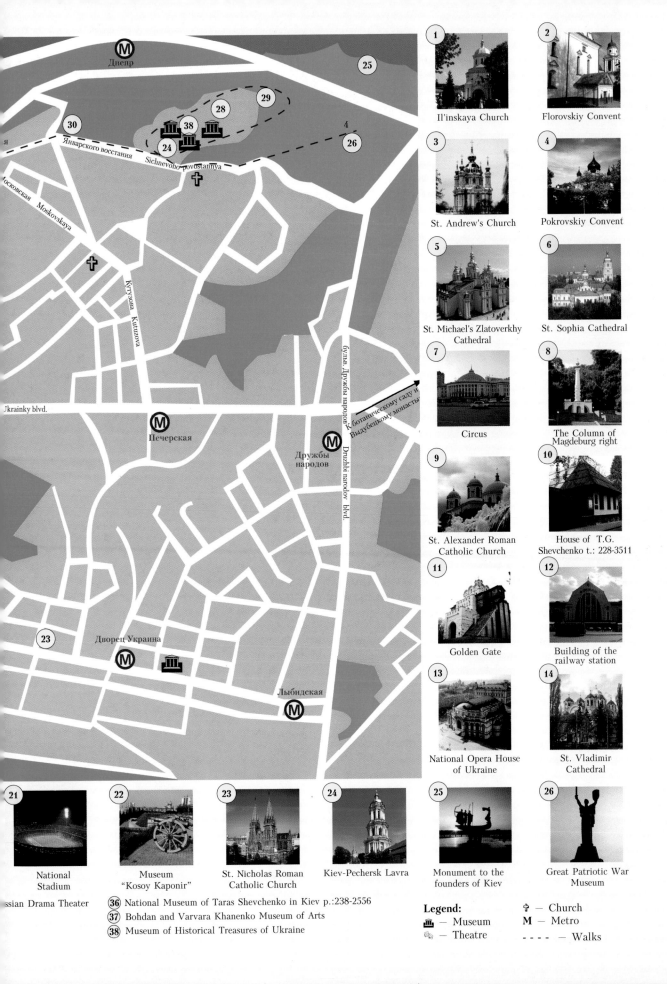

Map labels (Cyrillic/Latin):

Днепр

Январского восстания / Sichnevoho povostannya

Московская / Moskovskaya

Кутузова / Kutuzova

Jkrainky blvd.

Печерская

Дружбы народов

бульв. Дружбы народов / Druzhbi narodov blvd.

К ботаническому саду и Выдубецкому монастырю

Дворец Украина

Лыбидская

Photo legend:

1. Il'inskaya Church
2. Florovskiy Convent
3. St. Andrew's Church
4. Pokrovskiy Convent
5. St. Michael's Zlatoverkhy Cathedral
6. St. Sophia Cathedral
7. Circus
8. The Column of Magdeburg right
9. St. Alexander Roman Catholic Church
10. House of T.G. Shevchenko t.: 228-3511
11. Golden Gate
12. Building of the railway station
13. National Opera House of Ukraine
14. St. Vladimir Cathedral
21. National Stadium
22. Museum "Kosoy Kaponir"
23. St. Nicholas Roman Catholic Church
24. Kiev-Pechersk Lavra
25. Monument to the founders of Kiev
26. Great Patriotic War Museum

ssian Drama Theater

36 National Museum of Taras Shevchenko in Kiev p.:238-2556

37 Bohdan and Varvara Khanenko Museum of Arts

38 Museum of Historical Treasures of Ukraine

Legend:

✞ — Church

🏛 — Museum   M — Metro

🎭 — Theatre   ---- — Walks